20 Biblical Conversations About Money

Teach Your Teen to Manage Money

By Jennifer Rasmusson

Copyright © 2019 Jennifer Rasmusson

Independently published, January 19, 2019.

All rights reserved. No portion of this book may reproduced, stored in a retrieval system, or transmitted in any form or by any means - electronic, mechanical, photocopy, recording, scanning, or other - except for brief quotation in critical reviews or articles.

This publication is designed to offer advice and does not guarantee financial wealth. The author is not to be held liable for the financial outcome of any persons. If expert advice is required, the services of a competent professional should be sought.

ISBN: 978-1-794338173

Printed in the United States.

Dedicated to my beautiful children, their children, and their children's children. I hope you have success with money and find peace in all situations that come your way.

~~~~~~~~~~~~~~~~~~~~~~~~~~~~~~~

For I know the plans I have for you," declares the LORD, "plans to prosper you and not to harm you, plans to give you hope and a future. Jeremiah 29:11 (NIV)

Forward

During a conversation with my husband one day, he let me know that we could look forward to a significant pay raise in the next several months. Instead of getting excited, I froze in fear and began to panic. You would think I would be jumping for joy and praising God, but I was afraid! You see, he was already making a nice income and we were failing to manage what we had. What we had was debt, a lot of debt. A larger income, in my mind, was a set up for more debt and more guilt. So I began a journey to learn how to manage money God's way.

We discovered that we were spending a large percentage of our money on minimum monthly payments, which meant we didn't have any cash flow. A natural reaction to not having cash flow is to desire a larger paycheck. After reading several books, we found that it doesn't matter how much your income is. What matters is how much you keep of your income. If you spend your entire paycheck, you'll have nothing to keep or manage. It's very important that we teach our children how to manage whatever amount of money God gives them. The goal is to teach them how to manage a small amount while they are young, so that they can then manage a lot when they get older.

Our society has a confusing view of success and wealth. Americans make a habit of going into debt in order to look successful, but fail to prepare for retirement. Then add the fact that a large percentage of Americans look down on the upper class and want them to give all their money away. If we don't step in and teach our teenagers about money, they will be as confused as the rest of society. The only way to put the confusion to an end is to dive into the Bible and learn what God wants for us.

I recommend that you read each conversation with your teenager, study the given scriptures together, and then discuss any questions your child has. They are also welcome to read it on their own and study the topics online. The 'Show What You Know' section is intended to help your teen start applying the teachings right away. You may need to adjust (or help with) this section depending on your child's age.

I know how busy we are as parents and it's easy to lose track of time. Before we know it, our teen is talking about moving out. And all we can think is, "There's so much more I have to teach you!" The good news is that most kids ask for more advice even after they have left home. My hope is to help you talk to your teen or young adult about money and offer biblical guidance for a financially peaceful life.

Contents

A Message to Young Adults..9

Conversation 1 - Check Your Heart 11
    Show What You Know...20

Conversation 2 - Work Hard...21
    Show What You Know...25

Conversation 3 - Pay Your Bills...27
    Show What You Know...31

Conversation 4 - Pay Taxes...33
    Show What You Know...36

Conversation 5 - Budget Monthly..37
    Show What You Know...41

Conversation 6 - Say No to Debt 43
    Show What You Know...47

Conversation 7 - Don't Spend Foolishly......................................49
    Show What You Know...53

Conversation 8 - Give Often and Generously 55
    Show What You Know...58

Conversation 9 - Know Your Banking 59
    Show What You Know...62

Conversation 10 - Keep College Cost Low 63
    Show What You Know...66

Conversation 11 - Always Have an Emergency Fund (Savings).....67
    Show What You Know… … … … … … … … … … … … …....70

Conversation 12 - Beware of Loaning Money, Give Instead……...71
    Show What You Know… … .… … … … … … … … … … …...75

Conversation 13 - Combine Your Money Once You're Married…..77
    Show What You Know… … … … … … … … … … … … …...81

Conversation 14 - Buying a Home … … … … … … … … ….…83
    Show What You Know… … … … … … … … … … … … … 86

Conversation 15 - Keep Needed Insurances … … … … … … ….87
    Show What You Know… … … … … … … … … … … … ….90

Conversation 16 - Invest Wisely … … … … … … … … … …....93
    Show What You Know… … … … … … … … … … …....….97

Conversation 17 - Plan for Retirement Early … … … … … ……..99
    Show What You Know… … … … … … … … … … … … …..102

Conversation 18 - Save for Your Children's College Early …….…103
    Show What You Know… … … … … … … … … ….… … ….107

Conversation 19 - Baby Steps … … … … … … … … … … ….109
    Show What You Know… … … … … … … … … ….… … ….113

Conversation 20 - Financial Goals… … … … … … … … … ….115
    Show What You Know… … … … … … … … … … ….…..119

Further Reading List… … … … … … … … … … … … … …... 123

A Message to Young Adults

I wrote this book for my children. My hope is that they, and you, will venture into the world equipped to manage money. I've always told my children that life is much easier if you pay your bills. The truth is, there is much more to learn and know about money, paying bills is just a small part. I have always taken care of the finances for our household, but have recently come to understand the full picture of what God wants for us. Until now, money has always scared me. It scared me because I didn't believe that I should have any. I didn't believe I deserved anything nice. That is a dangerous place to be as an adult.

To help you with managing money, we need to first learn what God teaches. Jesus teaches more about money than any other topic! That's because Jesus knows that money is an issue of the heart. I hope that you have someone to talk to and ask questions. This book is designed to be a conversation starter between you and a parent, but you can also use it on your own. The scriptures are paraphrased, so please be sure to read them in your Bible. Let God speak to you through his Word. The 'Show What You Know' section is intended to help you start managing money right away. There is space to write in the book, but if you are a detailed writer you may want a separate notebook. I included a list of suggested books to further your study of money.

Something I want you to always keep in mind is that *how much money you make doesn't determine if you can gain wealth or not.* The average income in America is currently around $59,000 a year (2018). To some people, this isn't enough to satisfy their immediate goals. The truth is, if you manage your money correctly, you may end your working career as a multi-millionaire. On the other hand, if you spend every penny you earn, you will end your career broke. *The goal is to keep, or invest, some of what you make, and spend less than you earn.* This is the key to becoming a wealthy person someday, hold on to it.

If you don't have parents you trust to talk to about money, then find someone in your community or church that you can talk to. Make sure they are someone who knows God's word and they are clearly successful. Notice, I didn't say rich, but successful. There are wealthy people all around us that don't *look* wealthy. They drive used cars and wear blue jeans. They look like typical people at the supermarket. They are conservative spenders and great savers. They are people who are financially stable, planning for their future, and generously giving. These are people I consider to be financially successful and strive to mirror. Try to find one of these people to guide you.

People who look rich, sadly, are many times in massive debt and just pretending to be rich. Don't fall into this trap of wanting everything your neighbor has and going into debt to get it. This is not where God is leading you. God has great plans for you, if you follow him.

I pray you have a life of peace, love, joy, and financial success.

~Jennifer Rasmusson

Conversation 1- Check Your Heart

How do you view money? Who do you believe money belongs to? Why do you want money to begin with? What are your motives for becoming rich? Do you need to choose between God and money? These are all important questions to ask yourself before venturing out on your own.

Money is a big responsibility and requires making sure your heart is in the right place. Where you spend your money reveals your hopes, dreams, fears, and insecurities. Money is nothing more than a tool, but people begin to trust it instead of God. Money, like a car, is a vehicle to help you get to where you want to go. But money won't take you there by itself, you have to be the driver, or manager, of that money. Money will only do what you tell it to. *It has no power on its own.* You are the boss of your money. Don't let money scare you or cause you heartache. When you follow God's word you will find peace in your financial life instead of anxiety.

Dave Ramsey teaches us different views of money. We all fit into one of the three spirits of money, or attitudes, below. You will need to examine your heart to see where you fit. We all have spent time in each spirit of money, but hopefully, you will begin to recognize what is "of God" and what is not. The last spirit, the spirit of gratitude, should be the goal of every Christian! You can find more on this subject in Dave Ramsey's book, *The Legacy Journey*.

Spirit of Pride- This group of people believe that they have gotten where they are in life solely on their own, God had nothing to do with it. Every dollar, every raise, every bonus, and every paycheck is because of them, and them alone. They find their confidence in their riches and may do just about anything to look rich, act rich, and get rich. This group of people will struggle with finding contentment, as well. There is always a bigger house, a better car, another toy to buy. There is nothing wrong with wanting these things, but a person with the spirit of pride will chase wealth for the wrong reasons and maybe dishonestly. Their motive to becoming rich is to impress others, prove self-worth, or feed selfish desires. They may fall into the trap of trying to get rich quick. You may hear this group of people say things like:

"I worked hard for MY money, so I DESERVE to have what I want."

"Why would I give any of MY money away?"

"I can do whatever I want with MY money."

"God has nothing to do with my success, I did it all on my own."

Scriptures to Study:

- The world, and everything in it, belongs to God. (Psalm 24:1, Duet 10:14)
- God grants you wealth. (Duet 8:17-18)
- We work hard, but only God can bring the victory. (Prov 21:31)
- Hoarding wealth for greed doesn't end well. (Luke 12:18-20)
- God gives, and he also takes away. (Job 1:20-21)

- Hear the Lord and walk in his ways. (Duet 10:12-13)

Personal Notes:

Spirit of Poverty- This group of people either believe that money is evil, or that they are simply not worthy of having anything nice. It can be hard to tell why people live in the spirit of poverty. I, myself, truly believed I wasn't worthy of having money, because other people told me it was something I shouldn't have. You see, people who believe money is evil really like to pore on the guilt and shame if you do have anything nice. It can be quite confusing. Do they believe money is evil or are they simply jealous? Regardless of the motive behind the guilt trip, it is not biblical. God blesses the diligent. I have never heard of being blessed with poverty, have you? The spirit of poverty seems to be a common theme in American society today. People would rather cheer for Robin Hood (who stole from the rich), instead of cheer for the hard working businessman that earned his big house and also employs many other people.

      God calls us to be content in all circumstances, even in poverty. Most of us start out in life with a small paycheck and then over time we gain experience, knowledge, and proficiency in our job. If we remain diligent, we will be rewarded with pay increases. But until then, we need to learn to manage what we have and remain content. Apostle Paul tells us to be content in **all** situations and continue pressing towards "the goal." Paul's goal was to expand the Kingdom of Heaven, as should be ours, but God will give you many other goals in your life as well. Goals for yourself, your family, your career, and your spiritual life. If God blesses you with wealth, I hope you will give money to grow the Kingdom of God as well as except his blessing for you. Don't believe people who tell you that you shouldn't have nice things. God wants to bless his children!

      God doesn't look down on wealth, but God does warn us to not idolize money. Make sure your heart is in the right place before you are richly blessed. At the same time, make sure you don't judge the rich and fall into the trap of jealousy, or into the spirit of poverty, that says the rich should give everything away. We have no idea how much they are giving away. It's between them and God. It's easy to confuse the spirit of poverty with plain jealousy. Jealous people like to condemn the rich because they don't have as much money. When you give everything away at one time, there is nothing left to invest in the future. There would be no more money to employ you or your neighbors, either.

If you win $1 million dollars and give it all away, you will have given just that $1 million dollars away. If you give 20% of it away, spend 20%, and invest 60% you may be able to give away at least 10 times that over the course of your life! If you suddenly have a lot of money, be careful who you listen to. Put the money in a savings account for at least 6 months (while you decide what to do with it) and seek guidance from a financial advisor. You will hear people who live in the spirit of poverty say things like:

"I don't need anything more." *(Ask yourself: is this because they're content or because they're not worthy?)*

"Why would someone have such a big house?"

"You don't need that, you just need to be content with what you have." *(Guilt trip!)*

"I'm 'content' with a little, I can give everything else away."

"Giving all you have to the poor is godly."

"You're greedy to want more."

"How could he possibly justify having that nice of a car?"

Scriptures to Study:

- It is good to enjoy wealth. (Eccles 5:18-19)
- Be content in all circumstances. (Phil 4:11-12)
- Press towards the goal God set before you. (Phil 3:13-14)
- Godliness with contentment is great gain. (1 Tim 6:6-8)
- Can rich men enter the Kingdom of Heaven? (Luke 18:18-27) *Take note, it was commonly taught that it took riches to enter heaven. Jesus confused everyone with this message!*
- For I know the plans I have for you……(Jer 29:11)

Personal Notes:

Spirit of Gratitude- This group understands that God owns everything, including money. If you recognize that money is part of God's world economy, then you get the understanding that he is looking to "employ" people that will manage it well. If you manage the money you have poorly, why would God want to give you more? This viewpoint helps us understand why the poor stay poor and the rich get richer. There isn't any scripture in the Bible that supports taking the wealth away from the rich to create equal pay for everyone. There are many scriptures that say give to the poor, but none to support wealth sharing.

People with the spirit of gratitude also have their priorities in order. God comes first, above all else! It's easy to begin trusting your money and no longer relying on God to come to your aid. It's easy to forget who owns your wealth. Remaining in the spirit of gratitude will help keep your heart in line with God's word. Generosity is also an important element to staying grateful. When you give out of obedience and love, the selfish desires of your heart diminish. You will hear this group of people say things like this:

"Thank you, Lord, for all that you have trusted me with."

"I am a manager of God's money."

"I trust God to guide my decisions regarding HIS money."

"All that I am, all that I have, is because of the Lord my God who blesses me."

Scriptures to Study:

- You can't have two masters, you must choose to serve God or money. (Matt 6:24)

- The LOVE of money is the root of all kinds of evil. (1 Tim 6:10)
- Trust in the Lord, not your riches. (Prov 11:28)
- Love God above your money. (Luke 12:16-21)
- Where your treasure lies, there your heart will be. (Matt 6:19-21)
- All of Heaven and Earth are watching your choices. (Duet 30:19)
- When you are faithful with a little..... (Luke 16:10)

Personal Notes:

Personal Notes:

Show What You Know:

- Let's pretend you were gifted $5,000. With the knowledge you have today, what would you do with it?

- Quickly review the three spirits of money. Now, what do you think God wants you to do with your gift? Make a list of all the possibilities racing in your mind. What is your final choice?

Conversation 2- Work Hard

Your work place is your ministry. You are there for a reason, for a time, and for a season. Everyone is born with a tug on their heart or talents that call us. God has a purpose for all of us. Whatever your calling/vocation may be, God makes it clear we are to work diligently. We are all called to work hard. No matter your age, we are to continue working. Of course, work will look different to all stages of life and seasons. Lazy or idle men will never prosper, in fact, according to Apostle Paul they shouldn't even eat! Even if you are unemployed, you are still called to work while you wait for God's next calling/job. Whether you teach music lessons, paint houses, or cut wood, you can always find a way to bring in money.

While you are applying for jobs, also consider the benefits each job has to offer you. Entry level jobs, such as fast food restaurants, won't offer many benefits. As you get older though, you will naturally want to pick jobs that offer you paid vacations days, paid sick days, paid holidays, health care, retirement plans, and maybe even company cars. Not all jobs offer benefits. Start thinking about what type of work you want to do and how much secondary education it will take to get you there. Once you find a job that fits your personality and career goals, make sure you work hard. There are many people who are unemployed and would be happy to have your job. Don't get lazy on the job, work hard to impress your boss so you can move up in responsibility and pay.

If you find that you hate your job, find a new job before you quit your current one. Also, consider saving at least 2 months of expenses to help with the transition. Employers have different paydays and processes, so you may find yourself without money for the first few weeks. Another thing to consider is the switch in health care. It's typical for your new employer to have you wait 90 days before offering you their health care. That means if you need medical attention during that 90 days, you'll need to pay for it in cash.

Once you leave home, it will be up to you to support yourself and your family. Your parents don't have an obligation to take care of you past age 18. Any help they give you is out of the grace of their heart. Most parents want to help their kids out when they can. But, your parents need to also take care of themselves. They don't have as much time left to work as you do, they need to save for retirement. If they don't save enough, they may need to live with YOU once they have to stop working! Before you ask them for help, do your absolute best to take care of yourself. If you really need to borrow money, make sure you pay them back in a timely manner. Or, if you need to live with them, always pay them rent. It costs money to live and eat, even at their house. Before you leave home, make sure you are ready to manage your own money so you can truly be independent.

Scripture to Study:

- It is a blessing to enjoy your work. (Eccles 3:22)
- All hard work brings profit. (Prov 14:23)
- The lazy become poor, the diligent prosper. (Prov 13:14, and Prov 10:4)
- Work heartily, as for the Lord. (Coll 3:23)
- You reap what you sow. (Gal 6:7)
- If you don't work, you won't eat/Don't be a burden. (2 Thess 3:6-12)

- Rest for the weary. (Matt 11:28-30)
- Balance work and relationships. The story of Mary and Martha. (Luke 10:38-42)

Personal Notes:

Personal Notes:

Show What You Know:

- I'd like you to take some time to write down all your different skills. Write everything down. Include skills like building birdhouses, painting fences, sewing clothes, cooking, playing an instrument, lawn maintenance, cleaning homes, and babysitting. These are all wonderful skills to have and could make you money.

- Once you have written down all your skills, put together a resumé to help you find a job. You can find templates for resumés online or in Microsoft Word. You may want to put together two different resumés, one for odd jobs you can do in your neighborhood, and another one to find employment. To help you get started, look up the words below regarding resumés and write down the key phrases you want to use:

    Objectives:

Experience:

Qualities:

References:

- When your resumé is done, you will be able to present your skills with confidence to the people around you. Make a list of the people or places you would like to share your resumé with.

Conversation 3 – Pay Your Bills

This seems simple enough to follow, but you would be surprised at how often people mess this simple task up! Life happens and is very unpredictable. We can do our best to be good stewards of the money God gave us, but there are still times we come up short on money. This can happen when bills fluctuate, or change, each month. The power bill is a good example of this because it will be less in the summer and considerably more in the winter. Not only that, your paychecks will fluctuate depending on how many hours you worked or how many days were in the pay period. The best advice I can give to help with this problem is to always budget high. That way you have the money when you need it or have surprise money when you don't.

When you don't pay your bills on time the phone starts ringing off the hook. Say good-bye to peace and hello to stress! If you find yourself in trouble and know you won't be able to pay a bill on time or in full, then it's important you call that company to set up a payment arrangement. That will keep the phone quiet, peace in your life, and you'll have a better chance of not getting the service shut off. There may be times that turning off a service is the best choice, maybe for a short time. After a few months of not paying a bill, the company/creditor will turn your debt over to a Collection Agency. The Collection Agency has one purpose: to get you to pay the entire amount in full, today. They make money by getting you to pay up! Debt collectors can be ruthless and degrading, although new laws no longer allow them to be.

We all have times that paying bills gets difficult. The best way to approach times like that is to have a set priority. Many people make the mistake of not paying their rent, since it will save them the most money. But that just ends in eviction! That means you may get kicked out of your residence and need to live in your vehicle. In order to keep your address, you will have to pay it all the following month *plus* the current rent and any late fees! Life gets difficult when we can't pay all our bills. If this happens to you, I recommend paying your bills in this order:

1. *Rent or Mortgage.* This insures that you will never be homeless (God willing).
2. *Food.* You can reduce your food bill and get help, but eating is necessary.
3. *Power.* If it is Summer time, you can go without, but not in the winter.
4. *Car Payment.* Hopefully you won't have this. But if you do, you don't want to lose your mode of transportation.
5. *Car Insurance.* If you lose your license you may lose your job!
6. *Health Insurance.* Life happens even during tough times……
7. *Debts….*hopefully none!
8. *Extra Utilities,* like water or garbage. These utility companies are easy to work with and will set up payment arrangements with you. You may need to shut off the garbage service for a while, dump fees cost less.
9. *Entertainment.* If you're afraid you won't be able to pay rent, turn these off!
10. *Personal Luxuries.* The coffeehouse, local restaurants, and the Mall are places you will definitely need to stop giving your money to. These are the things that should be the first to go. If paying your bills is difficult, lifestyle changes may be necessary.

Scripture to Study:

- Repay your debts. (Psalm 37:21)
- Keep your word. (Num 30:20)
- Let your 'Yes' be 'Yes' (James 5:12)
- A good name (Prov 22:1)

Personal Notes:

Personal Notes:

Show What You Know:

- Ask an adult what bills they pay each month. Make a list of those bills and add them up.

- Take time to see how much apartments are in your neighborhood. Make a separate list of what you think you will actually be paying when you move out. Be sure to include car insurance, food, gas, and how much you want for spending. *You will use this in future Conversations.*

- Okay, now imagine having $300 less than you need because you got sick and your paycheck was cut short. What would you do? List the bills you would pay in order of importance. How would you make up the difference?

Conversation 4-Pay Taxes

There are two things people say are certain in life: death and taxes. The government wouldn't be able to provide roads, schools, emergency services and much more without charging taxes. That means that we need to contribute our share. Each year, between the month of Feb and mid-April everyone in the country files for federal income taxes. Most states also have a state income tax that is filed separately. You will need to check to see if your state is one of them.

According to Turbotax.com, if you make under $12,000 a year (2018), you don't need to worry about filing federal income taxes. If you make more than that, you need to file a 1040 form by mid-April. At a minimum, you must file every 2 years to avoid being charged with tax evasion, which is a federal offense (a felony) with jail time of 3-5 years.

If you make a mistake on your tax form or you're unable to pay taxes owed, you will not be at risk of going to jail. In that case the IRS will work with you, hopefully politely, to correct the mistake or make a payment arrangement for back taxes owed. Committing tax fraud (lying on your tax form) or refusing to pay what is owed is considered tax evasion. Telling the truth is definitely the best course of action!

With that said, you don't want to give any extra money to the government, either. We are much better stewards of our money than the government is. To help you with the filing process, you can find computer programs like Turbo Tax to file on your own. You can also go to IRS.com to file it directly. Or you can hire a certified accountant to do it for you for a fee.

When you are first employed at any job, you will fill out a W-4 form for the IRS. This way, your employer will be doing their part to be honest with how much they are paying you. You will also choose how many dependents you claim for taxes. If you claim 0, they will deduct the highest percentage they can from every check. This is definitely a bummer, but you may have a nice tax refund every Spring! You also have the choice of claiming a higher number of dependents, which means that less will be deducted from your check and will receive a lower tax refund. The government will also take out a small percentage for social security and other government services.

This is also the time you can let your employer know what percentage you want taken out of your check for your 401(k). A lot of companies are automatically taking out 3% to add to your 401(k) unless you tell them you want a higher or lower percentage taken out. You may also choose to have nothing taken for your 401(k), it's up to you. However, you don't have a choice how much taxes you owe at the end of the year or paying for social security and the other small fees they take out of your check.

Scripture to Study:

- Pay your taxes (Matt 22:21)
- Respect your government (Romans 13:1-7)

Personal Notes:

Personal Notes:

Show What You Know:

- Take time to view a W-4 form and a 1040 form online at IRS.com. Ask an adult if they would be willing to share with you one of their past 1040 forms. Your employer will send you a W-2 form every January that will help you fill out the 1040 form.

- While you are at IRS.com, you can learn about a Schedule C Form for businesses. The IRS offers tax write-offs for business expenses, but the rules change every year. What are some of the current tax write-offs?

- Remember to be patient with yourself while you learn, we all have a first time for everything. There are lots of people who would be willing to walk you through this process, or you can hire someone to do it for you. Who would you like to help you when the time comes?

Conversation 5- Budget Monthly

By definition, a budget is an estimation of income and expenses during a set period of time. That means, that each month or pay period we need to estimate how much we will get paid and how much we need to pay out. That is a very basic budget. I would like to teach you how to go beyond the basics and learn how to manage your money. Managing money starts with a budget. You need to have a list of all your expenses (bills) and a list of what you think you will need to spend in the future. To help you with this I created one for you below. You can also find many different expense trackers or sheets online. Working with an expense sheet is a great tool. Excel is the easiest tool I have found to create your own.

Budgeting doesn't mean you can't spend your money, it just means you are being wise with what God has given you and following a plan. A budget helps you to CONTROL and HARNESS your spending. Plan on budgeting each month for your whole life, even when you're wealthy, and even in retirement. Budget every dollar; each dollar needs to have a place or it will be wasted. How will it be wasted? It will simply be spent carelessly, without knowledge of how much you spent, or where you spent it!

I suggest breaking your budget up into 4 sections. The first one is Tithing. God makes it clear that we are to tithe 10% of our "first fruits" to him. That means it's the first thing we budget for. If we are living within our means, tithing should be easy. The next section is Living Expenses. This includes your bills, food, gas, and any debts. This is the total you NEED to pay out every pay period. Your home should be no more than 25% of your net income, 20% is better. The next section is your

Spending Plan. This is how you PLAN on spending your money in the future. This includes your clothing allowance, vehicle maintenance, dining out, vacations, birthdays, holidays, etc. If there is a big ticket item that you want to save up for, like a car, you would put it here. The last section is Investing. We cover the importance of this topic in Conversation 16. But for now, understand that this section is strictly for your future. This percentage should be used to save money for your Emergency Fund first (discussed in Conversation 11). When your Emergency Fund is complete, then use it to invest in your 401(k) or a Roth IRA. The percentages given below are flexible, but try to stay close to these numbers:

    10% - Tithing (to your church or local charity)

    50% - Living Expenses (home, utilities, food, gas, etc.)

    25% - Spending Plan (future spending and needs)

    15% - Investing (retirement) **After you have Savings**

    Using percentages while budgeting will ensure that you are spending within your blessing. If there is only 100 pieces (%) in your "pie" or pay check, then breaking everything down to a percentage will help you be the driver and manage your money. It takes a few months to get the hang of using a budget. So be patient while you learn. Most people feel amazed at how much spending money they have when using a budget. You will also find that you relax when spending money because you won't be worried about over spending. Budgeting sets you free and gives you peace-of-mind! Until you are married, it is recommended that you have an accountability partner that helps you budget monthly or at least brainstorm. Two minds are always better than one.

Scripture to Study:

- Count the cost and prepare. (Luke 14:28-30, Prov 24:27)
- Tithe 10% (Gen 14:19-20, Gen 28:20-22)
- Spend Righteously. Mary pours oil on Jesus's feet - worth $50K today. (John 12:1-8)

Personal Notes:

Personal Notes:

Show What You Know:

- Imagine you make $2,000 a paycheck. That would be a net income of $48,000 a year. (Net income is after taxes) Split your paycheck into the four sections explained above.

    Tithing 10% =
    Living Expenses 50% =
    Spending Plan 25% =
    Investing 15% =

- Next, fill out the Expense Sheet (found on the next page) with the bills that you listed in Conversation 3. You can also find an Expense Sheet online if you choose to use that instead.

- If you find that the amounts are too high, make adjustments to your line items in your Spending Plan. Maybe your Living Expenses need to be lowered to fit 50% of your paycheck. This is a skill you will need to have for budgeting each payday. Ask for advice from a trusted adult, they have the life experience that you need in this area. *You will use your Expense Sheet for future Conversations.*

Expense Sheet

Tithing 10% =

Living Expenses 50% =
Rent/Mortgage
Food
Gas
Power
Vehicle Insurance
Health Insurance
Other Insurance
Utility
Phone
Cable
Internet
Other
Other
Total:

Spending Plan 25% =
Entertainment
Vehicle Maintenance
Clothing
Other
Other
Other
Total:

Investing 15% =

Paycheck Amount: **Total Budget:**

Conversation 6- Say No to Debt

Debt is ANYTHING that is owed to another person, typically an agreement to pay someone (a company) back the money you borrow. The problem is debt makes you poor and credit card (CC) companies, or a bank, rich. They make money by charging you interest on your loan, while you struggle to pay it back. Banks and CC companies work hard at making you think they are offering you a great deal. What they aren't telling you is that they know, or are betting, that you won't pay them off quickly. The longer it takes to pay off your loan or credit card, the more interest you will pay them. The minimum payments they ask for each month may keep you in debt for decades! Offers of 0% down, 0% introductory interest rates, and bonuses like airline miles, are all traps that rarely work out the way we intend it. Stay away from bank loans and credit cards. Living debt free will give you financial peace in all situations. This is God's will for your life.

Many people believe that we have to use credit cards to establish good credit. Creditors like to use a number called the FICO score to decide if you are credit worthy. In order to have a high FICO score, you must be in debt. The truth is that credit cards will deplete your cash flow and steal from your future. It is simply not true that we have to use credit cards to make large purchases. There are banks out there that don't require a FICO score to give a mortgage loan, you just have to look for them. 25% of American adults are debt-free! To learn more about this topic, read Dave Ramsey's book, *The Total Money Makeover*.

Living debt free is no easy task in today's world, it requires checking your heart. The biggest reason people go into debt is because they are comparing themselves to others and want to keep up with "The Jones's." We compare ourselves to other people and "have" to have what they do. Playing the comparison game steals your joy and your paycheck, it's a costly game. Purchasing anything with a credit card is not being honest about your current income. If you have to buy something on credit, you're lying to yourself. You may be trying to make yourself look rich or more successful, or impatient for what you want.

Living debt free includes your vehicles as well. New vehicles depreciate the moment you drive them off the car lot. According to CarFax.com, a new car will lose 10% in value within 1 month of purchase, 20% in value within 1 year, and an additional 10% every year thereafter. Instead of buying a new car that eats your money so quickly, buy a used car (in cash) that is 3-4 years old. Save money while driving an older, used car and then trade up when you have more cash in hand. It may take several years, but imagine how fun it will be to walk into a used car dealership and buy your favorite, gently used, car in CASH! Say "no" to a $400+ monthly car payment and say "yes" to peace and joy!

<u>Save money four ways when you spend in cash:</u>

1. You save money when you don't have to pay any interest on your purchases.

2. You save money by receiving discounts. Car dealerships and retailers will give you a discount for paying cash, in-full, and on the spot for large items. Go prepared!

3. Spending in cash causes separation pain so you will naturally spend less.

4. Spending in cash won't steal your cash flow on monthly payments, which causes problems in the future and may cause you to go into more debt.

Be at peace with where you are today and keep pressing towards your goals. God wants to bless your diligence. Borrowing from the future doesn't bring the blessings and happiness you seek. You end up stressed out, full of anxiety, and broke! Pretending you're rich to please others isn't worth all the pain it causes.

Scriptures to Study:

- The blessing of the Lord makes a person rich, he adds no sorrow with it. (Prov 10:22)
- The borrower is a slave to the lender. (Prov 22:7)
- Do not borrow. (Duet 28:12)
- Do not ask for surety (co-signer) (Prov 22:26-27)
- Owe nothing but love (Romans 13:8)

Personal Notes:

Personal Notes:

Show What You Know:

- Living debt-free is a challenge for all of us, especially in the area of owning a vehicle. Let's make a plan to help you never have a vehicle payment. Let's write a plan to someday have a vehicle that costs $20,000 that we buy in cash! To do that, we are going to say you have $2,000 in the bank and don't have a vehicle yet. Fill out the Goal Sheet to show how many purchases it will take to get to your $20,000 car, it will take many. <u>Purchase 1:</u> Buy a used vehicle with your $2,000. Continue to save money while you drive that one. Save another $2,000. <u>Purchase 2:</u> Sell your current vehicle for as much as you can, let's say the same that you bought it for, so $2,000. Now go buy your second car for $2,000 plus the $2,000 saved, so for $4,000. Continue to save another $2,000. Keep repeating this process until you can buy your choice car for $20,000!

(Keep in mind that this is just one way to meet the goal of owning a nice car debt-free. You can also drive an older car for several years, repairing it when needed, and saving up until you have the desired amount of money.)

Goal Sheet

Purchase 1: Buy a car for $2,000
Save $2,000
Sell current car for $2,000
Purchase 2: Buy next car for $4,000
Save $2,000
Sell current vehicle for $4,000
Purchase 3: Buy
Save
Sell
Purchase 4: Buy
Save
Sell
Purchase 5: Buy
Save
Sell
Purchase 6: Buy
Save
Sell
Purchase 7: Buy
Save
Sell
Purchase 8: Buy
Save
Sell
Purchase 9: Buy
Save
Sell
Purchase 10: Buy

What vehicle do you plan on buying?

Conversation 7- Don't Spend Foolishly

Since you have learned how to manage your money wisely by budgeting, we are going to assume that you are only spending 25% of you income. That means that you are well on your way to being a responsible steward of God's money. Here's the thing though, even if you are only spending 25% of your net income, you may still be making some bad choices. Let's look at some of those choices.

The first one that comes to mind is gambling. Now, some Christians will tell you that playing cards or poker is a sin. I'm going to explain that a bit. I don't think the sin lies in the game itself. Drinking wine isn't a sin, but becoming drunk on wine is (Eph 5:18). Just like taking pictures is not a sin, but lusting after what is in the picture is (Matt 5:27-28). The sin is what happens in the heart while you gamble. When we gamble, our hearts immediately lust after money, which is a sin. Playing poker with candy keeps the game innocent and fun. Countless men have died for cheating during a poker game, because money was involved. Additional people have died from committing suicide after losing too much money. It's dangerous to get involved.

As a good steward of God's money, it's unwise to gamble your hard-earned money away. The truth about gambling is that we typically lose, that is how the casinos stay in business. They take our money because we willing give it to them. There are much wiser things we could do with our money. If you have money to give to the casino, why not invest it? Why not save for your next car? Why not save for a down payment on your first house?

Another thing to note about gambling is the addiction that may come with it. Gambling gives you a "high" if you win even a small amount. It has a way of sucking you in and getting you hooked. My father fell victim to this addiction, my parents ended up divorced because of it. Unfortunately, my dad never learned to keep his money. He continued to gamble and live in poverty until he passed away. The short answer is to keep your money and stay away from gambling.

Another way we spend foolishly is by spending in excess. We intend on spending just a small amount. But then we go out with our friends and without thinking we can begin to eat out all the time, buy coffee every day, and buy expensive clothes, since she did. Sometimes, we allow ourselves to buy high-end things, even though we can't really afford it. Dave Ramsey describes this as "Spending like Congress." Meaning, we aren't really paying attention to how much we are spending and then suddenly realize what a mess we have made of our finances! This is exactly why creating and following a budget is important. A budget will help us spend wisely and without worry.

I would also like to challenge you a bit in the area of spending. There are many things we want in life. The world shouts, "Buy me," everyday, everywhere we go. We have to learn to ask ourselves if we really want the things shouting at us. Many of us buy countless objects that clutter our homes and just end up at the local donation center. Before you buy anything, ask yourself, how long have I wanted this? How much should I spend on this? Is it wise to buy the expensive one, or should I buy the cheaper one? Is this item going to get used? If yes, how often? I recommend doing research before buying items such as vehicles, appliances, and electronics. Not only that, wait before you buy anything. If you truly want something, you will still want it a week from now or a month from now. *And always spend in cash.* If you have to use credit, you're not spending within your blessing. Buying in haste many times ends in regret.

How do you know if you aren't spending wisely? *If you aren't able to pay your bills or save for all your future needs, like car maintenance or clothes, you know something needs to change.* Make sure you are really being responsible with your spending. God does want to bless you, he will continue to bless you if you are a good money manager. Hopefully you will have some extra money each paycheck to go to the movies with your friends or eat out every once-in-a-while. Until you get the hang of not over spending, I recommend you budget with someone you trust to help you make decisions.

Scriptures to Study:

- Don't chase wealth and become foolish (1Tim 6:9)
- Keep your lives free from the love of money (Hebrews 13:5)
- Do not worry about tomorrow (Matt 6:31-34)
- The unrighteous will not inherit the kingdom of God (1 Cor 6:9-10)
- The greedy bring ruin to their households (Prov 15:27)
- Evil desires lead to sin, sin leads to death (James 1:14-15)
- Be on guard against greed (Luke 12:15)

Personal Notes:

Personal Notes:

Show What You Know:

- Let's work more on our Spending Plan. I want you to go back to your Expense Sheet that we used in Conversation 5. Take time to figure out how much you want to save in an entire year for your line items in Conversation 5. Then figure out what you want monthly for each item by dividing by 12.

- Let me help you with car maintenance. We know that we will need oil changes, we also know that tabs and registration will be due once a year. You will need new tires about every 3 years. Divide the total you need for tires by 3, so you will have what you need after 3 years of saving. Add everything up. Now, divide that total by 12 to save for it each month. How much do you need to save each month for car maintenance? You may want to add brakes and battery costs to this as well. This is how we manage our money wisely.

    Tabs and Registration Cost:

    Annual cost of oil changes:

    Tire Cost (for 4 or more for flats)

    Divided by 3 for annual cost:

    Add everything up and then divide by 12:

    Total Monthly Cost for Vehicle Maintenance:

- Once you have all of your line items broken down into monthly totals, split the amount in half if you want to know how much to save each paycheck.

- Refer back to Conversation 5, how much do you have for your Spending Plan each paycheck? Do you have any extra money for fun or planning a vacation? Are you wanting too much money for clothing or entertainment? This is where you learn to HARNESS your spending habits. As much as we like to spend, we also need to save if we ever want to be wealthy.

Conversation 8 – Give Often and Generously

Big hearts have big happiness! We are created in God's image and he loves to give. He has a heart full of love, mercy, and generosity. Because we are created in God's image, that means we are also created to give. We are denying ourselves a piece of our identity, or blessing, by not giving. Giving brings us joy. Giving steers us away from greed.

Giving can get quite addicting because it can be so fulfilling. Make sure you aren't giving TOO much, so much that God has to provide again for you. Also, you don't want to give away everything... unless God truly calls you to. Giving everything away is another way of telling God, "I don't want the responsibility of managing money, Lord, ask someone else to." Remember, God is looking for people who are willing to manage his money. If you invest now, you can give much more over your lifetime. Something to refer to is the Spirit of Poverty. Make sure you're not giving away all your blessings because you feel you don't deserve them. God wants to bless you too.

At the same time, make sure you are not shortchanging God or yourself by not giving enough. Tithing 10% to your church is a great place to start, the church needs us to do so. This again, is a matter of the heart. Remaining generous with your money will keep you from idolizing it. If you become wealthy, the percentages discussed in conversation 5 may need to change. You probably won't need 50% for living expenses, and you may want to give much more than 10%. Decide with God how much your Living Expenses should be, and all the budgeting ratios. It is no one's business how much you give or live on. Never let someone's jealousy steal your joy, and never accuse someone of not giving enough. You have no idea how much they give. You have no place of judging them, or them you. God loves a cheerful giver... give out of love. Remember, a generous heart remains in a spirit of gratitude!

Scripture to Study:

- Give to the poor (Prov 28:27)
- Give to the poor, God will repay you. (Prov 21:5)
- Give greatly, it will come back to you. (Luke 6:38)
- Give humbly (Luke 18:9-14)
- Give cheerfully (2 Cor 9:7)
- Give in Secret. (Matt 6:-1-4)
- You will receive tenfold when you give from the heart. (Gal 6:7)
- Give how much? The story about the scribes and the widow's mites. (Luke 20:45-21:4) *The widow gave all she had because people were told it took riches to enter heaven.*

Personal Notes:

Personal Notes:

Show what you know:

- Let's have fun with giving! Go back to how much money you had for giving in Conversation 5. How much do you have for tithing each paycheck?

- I know it can be boring to just write a check to your local church every two weeks for tithing. But, that's what God asks us to do. So, I want you to write a pretend check to your church, or maybe an adult will give you a real one of theirs to write. Or better yet, maybe someone will let you tithe for them at church next Sunday. If you already have a job, I encourage you to start tithing now. It may surprise you how it feels to give!

- Next, I want you to pretend that you had some surprise money come your way, $3,000. I want you to decide how to give this away. Will you bless someone at the grocery store who needs help? Give some of it to the widow next door? Maybe a charity like St. Jude? Or surprise a stranger by paying for their dinner? Have fun giving!

Conversation 9 - Know Your Bank

Banks are not all alike. They are like shopping for shoes. Your bank will be excited to have you, so it's easy to open an account. But why are they excited to have you? Because they make money by charging you fees! Banks charge different fees, some higher, some lower. Credit Unions are better than banks because they charge less fees and give higher interest rates for savings and investing.

You can have as many accounts as you want, at as many banks as you want. I have many saving accounts, one for each item I am saving for. That means I have one for clothes, one for Christmas, one for car maintenance, etc. You can also view and manage everything online. It's easy to learn how to even pay your bills directly from your bank to other companies. You can even set up your account to automatically transfer money to your savings accounts so you don't forget to save. Just remember, it's your job to manage your money. I recommend viewing your accounts online every couple of days to make sure you haven't been a victim of fraud. If this happens, call your bank or credit union right away.

You have to balance a personal ledger and watch your account balance. The bank won't tell you when you are overdrawn on your account (negative) but will be hasty to charge you a $35 fee. You have to know the fees they will charge and be aware that money mistakes get expensive, quick! Your bank will let you know when you open your account of all the fees they charge. Don't ignore reading what they give you. Ask them any questions you may have, the more the better. It's their job to be honest with you, but you have to ask. Always make sure that your bank is close enough to drive to, has many ATMs, and is FDIC insured to $250,000. I also recommend you buy checks. You may not think that you need a check book, but trust me, you will be glad you have checks. I still write about 3-5 checks a month to people.

Scripture to Study:

- Pay attention to your flock (money). (Prov 27:23)
- When you're faithful with a little…….. (Luke 16:10)

Personal Notes:

Personal Notes:

Show What You Know:

- Take time to visit a bank and open a savings account if you don't already have one. Learn how to use the ATM and your ATM card. Once you turn eighteen you will be able to open your own checking account with a debit card and checks. Until then, start saving for you first vehicle or college.

- Go online and learn what the fees are for a bank of your choice. Do the same thing for a local credit union.

    Bank:

    Fees:

    Credit Union:

    Fees:

Conversation 10- Keep College Low

Not everyone will need to go to college, it will depend on what you want to do. But remember, God rewards the diligent. Most careers will get a jump start faster if you get at least 2 years of secondary education. Maybe a vocational college is what you are looking for. Some careers will require 4 years, some even 6 or 8 years. Anything over 2 years will have to be done at an University, which costs a lot of money. But....which University is best for you? If you stay close to home you can cut down on living expenses by living with family. Does the school need to be an "Ivy League" school? Most likely not... unless you desire to go into politics. Where you choose to go will have a great impact on the cost. Private schools cost a fortune but offer the same degrees as a State University.

Work diligently to keep costs low. Apply for grants, financial aid, and scholarships. Getting good grades and a high SAT score may also help you with those scholarships. Whatever school you choose or for however long, work hard during school to help pay for tuition and books.

Ask your parents if they were able to save any money for your college tuition. Not everyone is able to do this. If you have to use a student loan, for a short season, work like mad to pay it off quickly. Student loans can be obtained through the school, which isn't paid on until your first job or within a year of graduating. *Never get a private loan through a bank or a credit card company because they will expect you to start paying them back right away.* Many kids have to drop out of college because they make the mistake of using credit cards.

Seek council from your parents, school counselors, and teachers on the best course for you to take. Your goal should be to keep your education as low as possible; you don't want student loans to rob you of your future.

A special note for girls or future wives: ask yourself how much college you really want to take. Do you want to stay home with your children? If the answer is no, than you will have plenty of time to work hard at your career and pay off any student loans. I believe women have a special place in the workforce and can be extremely successful. If you do want to stay home with your children, ask yourself how much education do you really want? Going to college for a couple years at a community college may be a great option. Even though you want to stay home, a couple years of college will benefit you and your family. But understand if you go into massive debt, you may have no choice but to work until that debt is paid off. You may not get the chance to stay home. Make your decision carefully and with advice from those you trust.

Scripture to Study:

- Seek Council (Prov 15:22)
- Obey your parents. (Eph 6:1-4)
- Provide for your household (1 Tim 5:8)
- You reap what you sow (Gal 6:7)

Personal Notes:

Personal Notes:

Show What You Know:

- Talk to your parents to see if they are able to help you with college expenses.

- Now, with that information in mind, start asking yourself what you really want to do for college. You don't need to decide what you want to do the rest of your life… you can change your mind. What general area do you want to study or learn about?

- Next, start visiting colleges or going to their websites to see if they offer a degree for your choice of study, called a major. Choosing a college that fits your educational needs and your financial needs can be a long process. Start now!

Conversation 11 – Always Have an Emergency Fund (Savings)

This is another difficult one. But the truth is, many of our "emergencies" aren't really emergencies. We know they are coming, we just don't know when. Some of them we can budget for in our Spending Plan, or some of them can be handled using savings. Savings will help you if you become unemployed, get in a car accident, wake up to a broken-down vehicle, or have unexpected medical expenses. This fund should be at least 3 months of Living Expenses, 6 months is even better. You may want to calculate some light spending into your monthly expense cost. You will still want to buy a pizza occasionally even if you're unemployed!

When emergencies come up, we will have a choice of going in debt to pay for them, borrowing (maybe even begging) from family, or we can simply dip into our Emergency Fund and take care of it! The third choice will give you peace because you can deal with each situation quickly and then move on. No fuss! If you have to go into debt, you will still be dealing with that emergency for months or even years to come. Yuck.

I know first-hand about going into debt because of the lack of savings. A misconception that many people have is that saving isn't needed as long as you have a large enough credit card to take care of it. The problem with this is we may not have the cash flow to pay off the debt. Then as life happens, we will have another emergency arise before the first one is paid off. This is an endless cycle of debt. Before you know it, you may have $30,000 of debt and contemplating bankruptcy.

Bankruptcy is when you go before a judge, say why you can't pay off your debts, and then they remove those debts from you. Sounds wonderful right? Not so much, it's quite embarrassing. Your credit score will fall very low for at least 7 years. Plus, righting off debts has long term consequences on our economy. This is a big problem. The bottom line is we need to plan for emergencies and pay any debts that we do incur. We just have to put money aside to take care of them when they do happen.

We don't want to admit that we may be unemployed someday, but it will most likely happen at least once in your life. Make sure you have enough money to survive and not lose your home. The 15% in your budget for investing should be saved until your Emergency Fund is complete. Once you have a desired amount of savings, go ahead and use that 15% for investing. When you use your Emergency Fund, take a break in Investing or Spending until it is built back up.

Scriptures to Study:

- Save for the time of famine. (Gen 41:47-49)
- The wise store up food. (Prov 21:20)
- Animals and Insects store up for the winter. (Prov 6-6-8)

Personal Notes:

Personal Notes:

Show What You Know:

- Okay, let's go back to Conversation 5. How much do you think you need to have in your Emergency Fund? If you lose your job, you will need to have this in place.

- Use the total you need for your Living Expenses and multiply that by the number of months you are comfortable with. It should be at least 3-6 months but more may be needed. What is your actual total?

- Now, using the 15% for investing that you calculated in Conversation 5, how many months will it take you to save up your Emergency Fund? Once this fund is complete you can start investing.

- Next, find a good account to save your money in. If you are over 18, I recommend a money market account or an online bank like Discover.com. You need to have immediate access to this money, so don't invest it.

Conversation 12– Beware of Loaning Money, Give Instead

Debts between loved ones can ruin relationships. If the relationship is not completely ruined, then it will at least be stressed. Debt creates guilt and shame for the receiver (because they feel embarrassed) and anger and frustration for the lender (because they aren't getting paid back). *It is better to just give.* Giving becomes a blessing for both parties involved. Finding a way to give anonymously to that person would be even better, then your gift would point to God! They wouldn't feel ashamed or embarrassed for needing money, as well.

Some people ask for money often, and large amounts. I recommend having a personal policy of never loaning a lot of money to friends or family. Tell them you value their relationship too much to risk losing it over money. Offer another way to help them or give them what you can. If they persist in needing a loan….remind them they don't need anything they can't buy in cash. If they need help with a vehicle remind them that they can always take a bus. Maybe you can give them a ride a few times. The hard fact is that some people would rather pay for a cell phone, a tall mocha from Starbucks, and eat out every day instead of saving the money they need to repair their current vehicle.

I hate to be so blunt, but lending money rarely ends well. Most often it ends in broken or strained relationships, and not seeing your money again. Instead of asking for your money back, just give it to them. Hopefully this will be appreciated.

Relationships are more valuable than the money in our pocket. If someone starts asking for so much that you risk not being able to take care of yourself, seek advice on how to set boundaries with that person.

I recommend to never co-sign for someone, either. The banks are dying to lend money, there is a reason your friend can't get approved. They will most likely not pay on time, every month. Your credit score will be damaged by the time the bank calls you to inform you they defaulted on the loan. Then it will be your turn to pay on the debt you didn't want and have nothing to show for it. After all… your friend is still driving the car you are now paying for. Don't make the mistake of taking on someone else's money issues.

Scripture to Study:

- Don't give surety (co-sign) to others. (Prov 11:15)
- Don't charge interest on a loan. (Ex 22:25)
- Give to those who ask of you. (Matt 5:42)

Personal Notes:

Personal Notes:

Personal Notes:

Show What You Know:

- Okay, for this Conversation I want you to go and talk to at least 5 adults in your life. Ask them about experiences they have had with loaning money to friends or family. Did it end well? Did it cause problems? Was the relationship strained if they gave them a loan? If you don't have an adult to talk to, you can do a web search on civil cases that ended up in court to settle disputes about money.

    Experience of Adult 1:

    Experience of Adult 2:

Experience of Adult 3:

Experience of Adult 4:

Experience of Adult 5:

Conversation 13 – Combine Your Money Once You're Married

There are some clear rules we need to follow before and after marriage. Even when we get engaged to be married, things may not work out or we may change our minds. If the relationship ends you will be crushed and won't want to deal with money issues. If you had begun to pay on your fiancés debt, you will probably never get that back. If you had combined accounts before the wedding, you will need to separate them and choose how to divide the money. If you moved in together before the wedding, you will need to separate all your belongings. I've seen a lot of couples move in together, and then break-up. Just don't live together before you're married. Young love typically isn't strong enough for the challenges that come along with combining your lives, space, and emotions. Not only that, you would be living in sin. Let's be real here, you won't remain sexually pure living in the same house for long. If your love is strong enough to face all the challenges, why not just get married? If you're not ready, then *keep your address and your money separate until after the wedding.*

While you're dating, be sure to have many open conversations about your personal beliefs. Talk openly about your views on Money, Sex, Religion, and Children. These are the top issues that cause divorce. You won't agree 100%. But, do you both want children? If yes, what religion you will raise them in? Do you both agree that saving is important? Does your boy/girlfriend have any debt? Student loans? How much? Is owning a home important? What do you believe about political issues? Pre-marital counseling will ask these questions and many more to help you determine if you really are compatible.

Once you are married, combine your money by getting a joint account with both names on it. Each person should have access to the money. All money earned, regardless of who makes more, will go into the family account and be family money. If your wife (or you) stays home, value her time and work with the children as you do your own work. She is working hard to raise the next generation right, that's more important than money. Everything you own is equally shared. No one gets less or more. Having a joint account will provide transparency and trust.

Talk about issues of financial infidelity: spending in secret with a plan to lie and/or hide it. (This is not the same as forgetting that money was spent) Financial infidelity can cause mistrust and also lead to divorce. Money is a big deal, we work hard to earn it. Treat it seriously and stay honest with each other in all areas, even money. Once trust has been broken, it can take a long time to rebuild.

Every month make a budget together, you may be able to have a templet to work from. Choose who will be the overseer of your money. According to Rachel Cruze, one of you will be a natural planner, the other a partier. The partier needs to be a part of creating the monthly budget, but probably won't care to watch the account every other day. *Once you have decided together, nothing can change unless you both agree to change it!* Make the budget the boss! Let the budget you created together help you make decisions through the month. Make sure you dream together while you are at it, dreaming is healthy. It gives you a purpose and direction. Dreaming together will keep you close. To learn more about this topic you can read Rachel Cruze's book, *Love Your Life, Not Theirs.*

Scripture to Study:

- Trust your spouse, for no lack of gain. (Prov 31:10-31)
- A prudent wife. (Prov 19:14)
- Two will become one. (Mark 10:8-9)

Personal Notes:

Personal Notes:

Show What You Know:

- Some people fight against the concept of marriage and choose to never get married because "it's nothing more than a piece of paper." For this conversation, I'd like you to prove them wrong. The first thing I'd like you to do is read at least 5 more scriptures about marriage. You can use the concordance in the back of your Bible or use the internet to find them. Ephesians chapter 5 is a great place to start.

Scripture and Message:

Scripture and Message:

Scripture and Message:

Scripture and Message:

Scripture and Message:

- Next, look up statistics on the health and well-being of married couples vs. single people.

- Last, do an internet search on the tax benefits for married couples. List your findings below. Now you will be ready to respond to all the negative comments you will hear!

Conversation 14 – Buying a Home

Buying a home isn't for everyone. It costs a lot of money and can be a source of stress and anxiety if you're not ready or don't want the responsibility of owning a home. Renting may be the best option for you if that's the case. A higher number of people are opting for this. Buying a home can also be a great long term investment and blessing if you are ready and prepared. In my opinion, renting is nice because the landlord has to fix everything as soon as it breaks.

Owning a home is also wonderful. You can make any changes to it, whenever you want. Plus, if you purchase your home at a good price, you may build up equity after a few years. If you are looking at your home as an investment, consider that you will want to live there long enough to cover all the fees associated with selling. There is a lot to learn about real estate. Make sure you learn from someone who is clearly successful and knows what they are doing. If you choose to buy a home, these are things I recommend you have before doing so:

1. Be debt free. You will have to adjust to a new payment that may be higher than you intended or thought. Your payment should be 25% or less of your net income.
2. Make sure you have a complete Emergency Fund saved up, including your estimated house payment. This should be at least $10-15K as a home owner.
3. Have at least a 20% down payment to pay in cash. This will take a while to save. Your monthly payments will be lower if you do this. Use the 15% for investing

to save up for your down payment, after your Emergency Fund is complete.
4. Only get a FIXED loan, no arms, balloons, are flexible rates. FIXED means the interest rate won't change over the life of the loan. You will save $100,000 or more if you get a *15 year loan instead of a 30 year loan*. Many people do "the impossible" and save up enough money by living on very little so they can buy their home in cash.
5. Once you are in your home, you will need to make repairs and improvements to protect your investment. Be sure to include this in your Spending Plan. You will want to budget for heating maintenance, septic maintenance, roof repair, etc.

Scripture to Study:

- Build you house on the rock. (Matt 7:24-27)
- By wisdom a house is built. (Prov 24:3-7)
- Ask for wisdom. (James 1:5)
- Listen to advise. (Prov 19:20, 12:15)

Personal Notes:

Personal Notes:

Show What You Know:

- Time to dream! This exercise should be fun. Go on to Zillow.com and find a house that you would like to buy some day. Write down the retail price of your chosen house.

- Look up the current interest rate that banks are offering for a mortgage loan.

- Go to www.mortgagecalculator.com online. Enter the price of the house and the current interest rate, then enter $0 for the down payment, and choose a 30 yr. loan. After it calculates the data, look to the right to see how much you will be paying in interest. Write that number down.

- Now, go back to the calculator and choose a 15 year loan. Notice how much money you will be saving in interest?

- Now go back again and enter a down payment of 20% of the retail price. The monthly payment and the total amount of interest is lower! How much did you save this time? Have fun playing with this calculator; Keep in mind that the numbers given are estimates.

Conversation 15 – Keep Needed Insurances

Why do you need insurance? The simple answer is for just in case. Just in case you get in a car accident. Just in case you break a leg or need surgery. Just in case you need glasses. Just in case there is a fire in your home. Just in case you die and leave your wife with children to raise on her own.

You will hear some people say that insurance is a scam and a waste of money. I disagree, car insurance is required to drive in most states. If you get in an accident, you will want to have your car fixed. Refusing to carry insurance will have some bad consequences. We all eventually need to use these insurances. You will be really glad that you have them in place when emergencies happen. *Emergencies will happen.*

Health insurance isn't required, but definitely recommended. There are health policies out there for people who rarely need to see the doctor. Honestly, even if you are extremely healthy, you should still have health coverage. Everyone is at risk of getting sick or breaking a bone. If you don't have health insurance and need to see a doctor, you will be responsible to pay for the visit, procedure, and medication in cash. It could add up to thousands of dollars.

There are many different insurances out there, some important, some a scam. Here is a breakdown that everyone should have. Like always, ask many questions and advice from those who are successful and have gone before you. Stay away from salespeople who are selling insurance, they may not be trustworthy.

1. *Car Insurance.* Most states require this as soon as you have a driver's license. As you grow in wealth and possessions you will want to get better coverage in case people sue you. Ask your insurance agent to explain the details of your coverage.
2. *Health Insurance.* This will hopefully come through your employer, but not all employers have a good plan anymore for the whole family. Depending on the insurance, you may be covered under your parents until you are out of college. You may also need to get your own health insurance as soon as you turn 18. Have your parents find out for you. You also need coverage for dental and vision, which are often purchased separately.
3. *Renters or Home Insurance.* Many renters skip this, but if there is a fire in your building the landlord won't replace your belongings. The bank will require this Insurance on a house until it's paid off.
4. *Life Insurance.* This isn't needed until you have a child. Make sure you get a Term Policy, there are many scams. If you don't use nicotine products it will be inexpensive! Chris Hogan recommended to have a life insurance policy up to 12 times the amount you make in a year. This way your family can replace your income if you die young.

Scripture to Study:

- Noah prepares for the flood. (Hebrews 11:7)
- The prudent sees danger. (Prov 23:3)
- The servant who knew his masters will. (Luke 12:47)

Personal Notes

Show What You Know:

- Insurance can be another overwhelming subject. Talk to your parents about your current Health Insurance and find out what age you will need to purchase your own policy. When the time comes, ask someone to help steer you in the right direction.

- For now, I'd like you to look into Vehicle Insurance. To begin, you can ask your parents where their vehicles are insured.

- There are different types of Vehicle Insurance, not all are required. Search the different types online before calling anyone, this will help you understand what you want.

    Liability Insurance:

    Collision Coverage:

Comprehensive Coverage:

Personal Injury Protection:

Uninsured Motorist Protection:

- Now, start shopping around to several different insurance companies to compare their premiums. You can also go to EverQuote.com to get quotes and compare premiums of all the major insurance carriers.

Conversation 16 – Invest Wisely

God talks a lot about investing. There is a right way and a wrong way to invest. Your income is the best way to slowly become wealthy, little by little. God warns us to not try to get rich quickly.

Trying to get rich quick leads to poverty, I have seen it happen. The stock market is a great example of this. If you put all your money in one stock in an attempt to make millions, you could lose all of it quickly, because you had ALL of it in one spot. Mutual Funds are a safer way to invest since the money is diversified across several stocks. Another way to end up in poverty is to use credit cards or loans to begin investing. It's a recipe for disaster and bankruptcy!

The best way to approach investing is with the "tortoise" mentality from the children's fable. The hare looks like he will surely win, but in the end the tortoise always does. Discipline and consistency are the key to success here. Frazer Rice taught us how to find a good investment in his book, *Wealth, Actually*. When you are deciding whether or not to invest in something, consider these four things before you do:

1. *Liquidity.* How quickly can I turn this into cash if I need it right away? Cash is the most liquid.
2. *Transparency.* How much information can I get about this, and how fast? Is the information public knowledge? Can I trust the source?
3. *Yield.* How much will I make over a long period of time?
4. *Impact.* What kind of impact will this have on my community or family? Negative or positive?

Make sure you seek help with investing before diving in. Your employer may also offer a 401(k) investment plan. Remember, God is looking for great money managers. Investing a percentage of your income every month will help you grow God's money, which will then allow you to give more over your lifetime. If you start young, you could retire with millions! Read, *Everyday Millionaire*, by Chris Hogan to learn more.

Scripture to Study:

- Wealth gained hastily will dwindle. (Prov 13:11)
- Get rich quick leads to poverty. (Prov 21:5, Prov 12:11)
- Parable of the Talents- 1 talent is $500k today. (Matt 25:14-30)
- Wisdom is with the aged. (Job 12:12-13)
- Listen to advise. (Prov 19:20, 12:15)

Personal Notes:

Personal Notes:

Personal Notes:

Show What You Know:

- For this Conversation I'd like you to visit Chris Hogan's website. Go to www.chrishogan360.com. Choose 'Articles' at the top of the home page. Next choose 'Money.' You will find many articles to read that will begin answering all your questions. Read at least 3 articles that interest you. Write down any questions you may have and ask a trusted adult. Be careful who you take investment advice from though, not everyone is educated in investing. Chris Hogan is someone we can trust to steer us in the right direction.

    Article 1:

Article 2:

Article 3:

Conversation 17 - Plan for Retirement Early

I know retirement seems an eternity away... but it's not. You will have about 40 years to work, but will live for 60-70 years. Meaning, you will live 20-30 years in retirement (hopefully) *with little to no income.*

The government will take a small portion of your check to pay for current retired people in our country, and then promise to give you social security when you retire. What they don't tell you is that it's not much, and at risk of being taken away. The retirement age for people born after 1954 is 67 (as of 2019). Which means you can't collect any social security until that age, but you may need to retire earlier for health reasons. And you will definitely need more than they give you. The average social security check today is $1,372 a month (2018). You will be lucky to get that much, and it won't be worth what it is today because of inflation! The best way to look at this issue is to plan on getting nothing from the government. If you receive social security during your retirement, then it will be a bonus!

So how do you save for retirement? If you start young, it will be easy. If you wait, like we did, it will be painful. Most employers will offer a 401(k) to help with retirement. They will take a small % of your check to put directly in that account. Your 401(k) is typically mutual funds in the stock market. You can contribute as much as $19,000 (2019) a year into this account, tax free, but you can't touch it until you are 59 ½ or you will lose 40% of it in penalties. Starting a Roth IRA is another great way to invest....it is a bit different because you have to contribute to that yourself. The great thing about a Roth IRA is that your money will be TAX FREE when you pull it out during retirement. The money in your 401(k) will be taxed as income during retirement as you draw money from it.

These 2 investments could make you very rich by retirement! Like I said above, you want to put 15% of you income to investments. When you are young, even $100 a month will be good. The investment will grow with compound interest, which takes time, the more time the better. I kick myself every time I see how much money we "lost" by not starting young!

As you get older, by 30, you will want to meet with an adviser to make sure you are on track to have enough money for retirement. The amount of money you want for retirement is different for everyone. Chris Hogan tells us that retirement isn't an AGE… it's a financial NUMBER. How old will you be when you retire? Trust God to meet your needs, even in retirement. To learn more, read *Retire Inspired* by Chris Hogan.

Scriptures to Study:

- Leave an Inheritance to your grandchildren. (Prov 13:22)
- Abraham leaves everything to Isaac. (Gen 25:5-13)
- Every tribe, or family, shall keep its own inheritance. (Num 36:9, Ezek. 46:6)

Personal Notes:

Personal Notes:

Show What You Know:

- I know retirement seems like it will never happen. The truth is, it comes faster than you think it will. If you start saving young, you'll have nothing to worry about. Go back to www.chrishogan360.com. This time click on 'Tools' at the top of the home page. You will find a link titled R:IQ Assessment. Enter an email to get started. You will then be directed to answer a few questions about your dream retirement. After that, a retirement calculator will appear. Have fun putting in different amounts to see how much you should save each month starting at age 21 and retiring at age 67.

Conversation 18 - Save for Your Children's College Early

We didn't start saving when our kids were little. We simply couldn't spare any money. It's difficult to do on a small paycheck. But even saving $50 a month per child will add up to $10,800 after 18 years (0% interest return). That's a nice gift to be able to bless your children with. Are your parents able to bless you with financial help for college? If the answer is yes, make sure you are truly grateful for their sacrifices. If the answer is no, you will soon understand why. Not everybody can afford to save up for their child's college.

If you are able to help your children, there are a few different programs you can invest in to help. Each state has its own program, some are better than others. You can invest in any state program across the country, not just your own. If you do use a state program, then be aware that the money has to be used for education. So, you run the risk of losing the money, or needing to pass it to another child, if your children don't go to college. Make sure you do your homework. An interest bearing account, or other investments might be a good idea, too. Whatever you do, start as soon as your child is born!

Lastly, make sure your retirement plan is in place before you start saving for your child's college. Why? Because they have time to pay on student loans, but you don't want them to have to take care of **you** when you retire. You may not have enough time to raise them, pay for their education, and then start thinking about retirement. By then you may be 45 or *older*….follow Dave's Baby Steps to make sure everyone, including you, is taken care of.

Scripture to Study:

- Save for your children (2 Cor 12:14)
- Teach children the way they should go. (Prov 22:6)
- Teach children God's Word. (Duet 11:19)
- Listen to your father. (Prov 1:8-9)
- No greater joy….(3 John 1:4)
- Discipline your children. (Prov 29:15-17, Prov 13:24)

Personal Notes:

Personal Notes:

Personal Notes:

Show What You Know:

- If you already have a child, begin looking into state savings programs. Read through the restrictions and benefits. You may also decide to save for your child's college another way. Either way, make a plan to put into action when you are ready to start saving.

- Next, I'd like you to spend time playing with compound interest. Find a compound interest calculator online and have fun playing with the numbers. Change the amount you save each month, change the interest rate, and change the length of time. Mutual Funds could give you an average return of 10-12% a year. How long will it take you to reach $1,000,000 if you save $100 each month? $150 a month? $200 a month? The important thing to understand about compound interest is that the magic is in the length of time. The more time the better!

- The last thing I want you to do is to go back to the 'Show What You Know' section in Conversation 1 and decide how you would spend that $5,000 now that you have learned how to manage money. Would you do anything different? Write out your plan and share it with your parent.

Conversation 19 - Baby Steps

Just like learning to walk, we all have to start with baby steps. It takes time to learn about money, it also take time to learn how to manage it. Dave Ramsey created 7 Baby Steps to help people take control of their money. If you want to win with money, I recommend following his Baby Steps. They are great for anyone at any stage of life. You can find them in detail in his book, *The Total Money Makeover*.

These steps assume you are in debt and in need of financial help, but we can look at his steps a different way. We can look at them as a PRIORITY for financial planning. You will have many goals in your life. The question is, when is the right time to buy the things you want? When do you buy a house? When do you start saving for retirement? What about the shop you want in your backyard? How do you squeeze your dream vacation in there before you turn 50? What if you get yourself in trouble and go into debt? What do you plan for FIRST? We can trust these Baby Steps to guide us. *Use these steps and the Budget in conversation 5 to accomplish all your financial goals.*

Use your Spending Plan to save up for anything you want. Remember to always pray first and make sure your desires are still in line with God's plan! The best way to achieve steps 1-3 is to use the 15% for investing and any other money you can spare. If you are debt free, you get to skip step 2. If you are in debt, you may need to make some life changes so you can throw as much money as possible at your debts. You can also attend one of Dave Ramsey's Financial Peace University Classes at a local church. He also has his own radio show that you can listen to daily or visit his website at DaveRamsey.com.

Baby Step 1: Save $1,000 as fast as possible. This is your baby Emergency Fund. Keep it in your savings account, don't spend it. This is enough to hopefully help you not go into debt any further.

Baby Step 2: Pay off any and all debts (except the house) as fast as you can. This may take a few months, it may take a few years. Line debts up in order least to greatest. Pay the minimum payments on everything until the first one is paid off... then roll the minimum payment of the first card up to the min payment of the second. You are adding the minimum payments of the paid off cards to the next debt you are focused on paying off. This is called the debt snowball. If you have to spend any of your $1,000 from step 1, take a break on step 2 until the money is replaced. Then return to step 2.

Baby Step 3: Finish Saving up your Emergency Fund. This should be 3-6 months of Living Expenses. Only use this for EMERGENCIES! This is your nest egg in case you lose your job. This will also help keep you out of debt. If you are wanting to buy a house, save for your down payment after you are done with baby step 3, but before step 4. The more you save the better, even 100%!!

Baby Step 4: Start Saving for Retirement. This step doesn't take long. Adjust your budget to include 10-15% of you income for retirement investing. Refer to Conversation 5 on budgeting to help you. Put enough in your 401(k) to meet your companies matching offer, then put the rest of the 15% towards a Roth IRA. You can contribute up to $5,500 a year per person (2018). When you spend any of your Emergency Fund, you will need to take a break from step number 4 and 5 and go back to step number 3.

Baby Step 5: Save for your Child's College. This is after retirement planning for a reason. The child has plenty of time to pay off debts, you won't have as much time to plan for the future. So after baby step 4, you can decide how much you have to invest out of your Spending Plan towards you child's college. Anything helps, it doesn't have to be all of it. You are NOT obligated to give your children money after they are 18. If they need help because of an extreme hardship, help them, but don't let them be entitled and don't enable them if they are simply refusing to work.

Baby Step 6: Pay off your mortgage! Steps 4 and 5 are pretty easy to set up. Now take a moment to make a plan on how to pay off your mortgage. Once your mortgage is paid off, you will be 100% debt free and will owe nothing to anyone!

Baby Step 7: Become Wealthy. Invest any and all extra money you have in future retirement or giving. Grow your money for the kingdom of God. Grow your money to bless your community. Grow your money to give to your family as an inheritance. Read *Everyday Millionaire* by Chris Hogan to learn how you can achieve this goal.

Scripture to Study:

- Time for every season. (Eccles 3:1-8)
- Trust in the Lord with all your heart. (Prov 3:1-12)
- Be still before the Lord. (Psalm 37:7-9)
- Don't grow weary. (Gal 6:9)
- Don't grow anxious. (Phill 4:6)

Personal Notes:

Personal Notes:

Show What You Know:

- Make a list of the things you want to buy in your life, I know this might be a long list. Time to dream again!

- Once your list is complete, review Dave's Baby Steps. Design a plan that includes all 7 Baby Steps and the things you want to purchase. My hope is you will start to set priorities and goals for your financial life. The step-by-step outline on the next page will help get you started, but you may need more space. Do you think you should buy your first car before or after Baby Step 1? Do you think you could go on a big vacation before or after Baby Step 2? After what Baby Step should you buy your first house? Remember, you will want to use the money in your Spending Plan (from Conversation 5) to save up for your purchases.

Baby Step 1:

Purchase:

Purchase:

Baby Step 2:

Purchase:

Purchase:

Baby Step 3:

Purchase:

Purchase:

Baby Step 4:

Purchase:

Purchase:

Baby Step 5:

Purchase:

Purchase:

Baby Step 6:

Purchase:

Purchase:

Baby Step 7:

Purchase:

Purchase:

Purchase:

Conversation 20 - Financial Goals

It is necessary to have goals if you want to achieve wonderful things in your life. I'm hoping you have many goals and dreams at this stage of your life! I remember how excited I was to announce myself to the world and do amazing things. Money is just one part of your life. We focus on many different areas:

- Social
- Heath and Exercise
- Romance
- Finances
- Business or Work
- Family
- Spiritual
- Personal Development
- Fun or Hobbies

All of these areas are important to grow yourself in. It's a good idea to set new goals at the beginning of every New Year. If we don't, we will fall into the habit of dreaming our life away, never really accomplishing anything. *That's because dreams don't take any work or effort!*

When we take the time to put our dreams on paper, we have more of a chance of making them come true. I have a small book I call *My Dream Book.* It doesn't have any words, just pictures. Pictures of everything I want to accomplish. I made a point of looking at that little book once a day for about a year. After a while, I forgot to look at it; eventually it was stuffed to the back of a drawer.

I made that small book almost 8 years ago. I was recently looking through it, and to my amazement just about ALL of the pictures in that small book had come to pass! There is power in putting your dreams on paper. You can make posters, book covers, journals, screen savers, or sticky notes for the mirror. It doesn't matter. Just write those dreams down, and put them somewhere you will frequently see them!

If you want to make your own dream book, start with a blank journal. Then, cut out pictures or print images that represent the things you want to accomplish. Make sure there aren't any words. Words will take your attention away from the pictures. No dates, no numbers, no words! Now, paste together your book and keep it at your bedside. Last, make a point of looking at it at least once a day. Here's the most important part: *make sure you VISUALIZE yourself living in that picture!* Visualization is absolutely necessary! One day while you are looking through your dream book you will realize that many of the pictures have become a reality in your life.

In order to accomplish our dreams we have to set goals. *Goals are step by step plans to achieve a dream!* A dream without a goal is nothing more than a wish. All the pictures in my dream book had to have goals attached to them (not in the book, though). Some goals take years to achieve. One of the pictures in my dream book was a house. Our house wasn't a gift, we had to work hard to make it possible. We didn't win the lottery or inherit a fortune. It took years of saving, planning, and preparation. We talked about it for years, setting ourselves up financially to be able to afford it. Goal setting will help you accomplish whatever God puts on your heart to achieve. There are countless books on the market about goal setting and achievement. I encourage you to find one of those books and be the *driver of your life*, not just your money.

We only have one life. One life to live to the fullest. One life to choose Christ. One life to love those around us. One life to win with money. One life to achieve whatever God sets before us. I hope you make the most of your one life.

Scripture to Study:

- Press towards the goal God set before you. (Phil 3:13-14)
- Choose life (Christ). (Duet 30:19)
- Think positive. (Phil 4:8)
- Power of life and death. Watch what you say… (Prov 18:21)
- Run the race to win. (1 Cor 9:24-27)
- God is your strength. (Isaiah 40:31)
- I can do all things……(Phil 4:13)

Personal Notes:

Personal Notes:

Show What You Know:

- To finish the last Conversation of this book, I'd like to encourage you to simply set goals that you would like to accomplish in 1 year, 5 years, 10 years, and 15 years from now. *Wow, 15 years from now, you ask?* Yes. In 15 years you will be between 30-35 years old. Someday you will look back on this book and either smile... or be disappointed. You will smile if you have already accomplished some of your goals, or you may be disappointed in yourself if you have let too much time slip by without direction. Be the driver of your life, today.

Financial Goals for 1 year from now:

Step by step plan to achieve these goals:

Financial Goals for 5 years from now:

Step by step plan to achieve these goals:

Financial Goals for 10 years from now:

Step by step plan to achieve these goals:

Financial Goals for 15 years from now:

Step by step plan to achieve these goals:

Further Reading List

Cruze, Rachel, *Love your Life Not Theirs.* Tennessee: Ramsey Press, 2016.

Hogan, Chris, *Retire Inspired.* Tennessee: Ramsey Press, 2016.

Hogan, Chris, *Everyday Millionaire.* Tennessee: Ramsey Press, 2019.

Ramsey, Dave, *More Than Enough.* New York: Penguin Group, 2002.

Ramsey, Dave, *The Total Money Makeover.* Tennessee: Nelson Books, 2013.

Ramsey, Dave, *The Legacy Journey.* Tennessee: Ramsey Press, 2014.

Ramsey, Dave and Cruze, Rachel, *Smart Money, Smart Kids.* Tennessee: Ramsey Press, 2014.

Rice, Frazer, *Wealth, Actually.* Lioncrest Publishing, 2018.

Orman, Suze, *The Money Class.* New York: Spiegel and Grua Trade Paperbacks, 2012.